WHO   IN CONTROL
OF THE CHURCH

A GUIDE TO UNITY AND PEACE WITHIN THE CHURCH

DR. JOHN ADAMS
DR. GAYLE ALEXANDER

DEDICATED IN LOVE AND APPRECIATION

TO

OUR FAITHFUL WIVES
ROBBIE ADAMS AND KELIEA ALEXANDER

WHO HAVE BEEN BY OUR SIDES THROUGH
ALL THE JOYS AND CHALLENGES
OF MINISTRY

Endorsements

"This book should be read by every pastor and church leader."

Don Wildmon, Founder of American Family
Association and Methodist Minister

I read with great interest "Who is Control of the Church" written by my former students and friends Dr. Gayle Alexander and Dr. John Adams.

Four things came to mind after reading the book. It is thoroughly biblical from start to finish, comprehensives in its scope, and thorough in it treatment. Fourth, these are truths the authors have learned both from the bible and from being themselves "in the trenches" in pastoral ministry.

I could not keep from agreeing with their conclusions in the five parts of their treatment. I believe preachers, of whom I am one, need to be more sensitive to the biblical principles of authority presented in this book. Doing so would make us more genuine <u>pastors</u> and true <u>servants</u> of the Lord and thereby solve a host of problems in the church.

Dr. Hyran E. Barefoot, fourteenth president
of Union University, Jackson, Tn.

This is a great book! Every preacher and Christian should read it. Among other great truths, it teaches that every pastor should have a divine call from God and be a true man of God, the church should be led by the Holy Spirit in the calling and treatment of their spiritual leader and all Christians should love one another from the bottom of their hearts. These truths, plus the others taught in this book, will lead to unity and peace in the church. I recommend that all lay leaders and pastors read this book!

Mr. Curtis King, businessman, layman and CEO of
King Tire Company, Jackson and Humboldt, TN.

"John Adams and Gayle Alexander have become a strong voice for honoring God-called servants who leave all to follow Him. I welcome their book and pray God gives it wide distribution and a great reception!"

Dr. Joe McKeever, Career Minister and retired
Director of Missions for the New Orleans Baptist Association

"This book allows the Bible to speak about strong shepherd style leadership by the pastor for the benefit of the congregation that makes for harmony and peace."

Roy Jones, Career Minister and retired
Director of Missions, Cape Girardeau, Missouri

Part one on pastoral authority is insightful and most beneficial. Authority conferred and earned would help all pastors. I especially found the material on the concept of double honor to be most helpful and insightful. Congregations would be well served to read this book and the treatment of their biblical responsibility toward their pastor.

Dr. Roger Stacy, Director of Missions, Trenton, Tennessee
"Over 100 years of combined service in the local church qualify John Adams and Gayle Alexander to write this book which contains a wealth of Bible teaching. The family of faith and the pastor need the instruction and counsel of this book more now than ever before. I hope it is well received and much used."

Dr. Bobby Douglas, Lifelong Minister of the Gospel
and Director of Missions

CONTENTS

PREFACE

INTRODUCTION

PART 1: SOURCES OF THE PASTOR'S AUTHORITY

PART 2: THE CHURCH'S BIBLICAL RESPONSIBILITIES TO ITS PASTOR

PART 3: THE PASTOR'S BIBLICAL RESPONSIBILITIES TO THE CHURCH

PART 4: THE MOTIVATION NEEDED TO OBEY GOD'S AUTHORITY

PART 5: A GLIMPSE OF THE BEAUTY OF UNITY AND PEACE

Preface

Several religious journals have reported that the terminations of many ministers have been caused by confusion over the authority of the pastor. For example, one survey cited the most common cause for firing was "control issues regarding who will run the church." Another study indicated the issue of forced resignations and terminations is a problem that transcends denominational lines.

An article appearing in *SBCLIFE, Journal of the Southern Baptist Convention* reported, "Hundreds of pastors and staff will be terminated this year with full time pastors twice as likely to be fired as bi-vocational pastors." Who is in control was listed as the number one cause for this problem.

Another search found that 28 percent of ministers said they had at one time been forced to resign due to personal attacks and criticism. Nearly 600 ministers responded to a survey by *Leadership* magazine, a journal for church leaders, published by *Christianity Today*. The findings revealed that 23 percent had been fired or forced to resign. One survey indicated that nearly half of the ministers terminated never reentered the ministry.

However, as revealing as these studies and surveys are, they do not commence to reveal the emotional, physical, and spiritual consequences of termination. These include grief, hurt, disillusionment, agony, and sadness. The pastor and the congregation's reputation in the community and beyond are involved. The pastor's family is harmed immeasurably as are many dedicated believers. Then, there is the spiritual dimension of termination. Mature and immature believers, as well as lost people, are adversely affected. Some forever! It may take generations for a congregation to get over the trauma of terminating her pastor.

The purpose of this study is not to bring an indictment of shame and disgrace to the faith community, although there is ample evidence to do so in many instances. Satan must be personally satisfied and jumping with glee with his successes in stopping the forward movement of the church with the devastation of terminating pastors.

This study provides solutions to the terminations of ministers and especially as it relates to authority. The purpose of this book will be to discuss the conferred and earned authority of the pastor, the church's biblical responsibilities to the pastor, and the pastor's biblical responsibilities to the church. A vital part of our purpose will be a discussion of the motivation needed to obey and respect this authority. Of importance to the purpose is providing the reader a glimpse of what obedience and respect for God's authority looks like: the beauty of unity and peace.

The principles presented here reflect the heart of God for His bride. These principles have been used faithfully over the centuries by God's people and have proved to be exceptionally effective. The biblical principles will be helpful to pastors and staff search committees, deacons, elders, and similar entities, pastors and priests, church leaders and members, denominational leaders and especially spiritual leaders and congregations with histories of power struggles.

The burden of this book is to prevent problems and conflict from arising between pastors and churches. The authors have not addressed plans and procedures for the resolution of conflicts.

<insert image 062.jpg>

Introduction

Understanding the place of authority in the church depends on a proper understanding of the church itself. A lack of comprehension of the nature of the church often leads to disorder and chaos in the fellowship. For this reason, we have included a brief presentation on the nature of the church, which includes both spiritual and practical aspects.

The spiritual dimension understands the church as a living organism. It is composed of redeemed people committed to loving Christ Jesus, one another, and all mankind. In Ephesians 4:25, the church is described as the perfect body of Christ. The Greek word used to describe this body is *koinonia*. As a community of believers in fellowship with Christ, it is ideal. In 2 Corinthians 1:2-8, Paul wrote, "Unto the church of God which is at Corinth, to them that are sanctified in Christ Jesus, called to be saints, I thank my God always on your behalf, for the grace of God which is given you ... That in everything ye are enriched by him, in all utterance, and in all knowledge ... that ye may be blameless in the day of our Lord Jesus Christ." The church has been made holy only by Christ's work of atoning on the cross of Calvary. Believers are in Christ, and this alone places them in a state of holiness. Only by being "in Christ" are believers made holy.

However powerful the spiritual aspect of the church may be, demonstrating that power to the world requires organization and structured leadership. The practical dimension of the church must be just that, practical. It is structured, elects leaders, governs itself, and has an approved leader, the pastor. Churches must have hands and feet to do their work of ministry. Most churches are highly structured and carry on their work through committees and various organizations, such as Bible classes, training units, music programs, mission education programs, a deacon body, and business meetings. The church must develop leadership roles and lines of authority to accomplish its work. God has already established the role and lines of authority for the spiritual leader.

It is at this point that many problems within the body of Christ may occur. At the root of most problems is a disregard for the distinct lines of authority that God has set for the church, especially in regard to its spiritual leader. Since the Bible dictates those lines of authority, the order within the church must be safeguarded by all concerned.

Sources of the pastor's authority

Authority that is conferred

Authority conferred by God's call

The divine call is the conferral of God's authority on a man. The Bible teaches that God calls men to preach and to minister. First Corinthians 11:1 reads; "Paul, called to be an apostle." In Romans 10:14, Paul asserts, "And how shall they hear without a preacher? And how shall they preach except they be sent?" In Ephesians 1:1, Paul writes, "Paul, an apostle of Jesus Christ by the will of God." Amos declares in 7:15, "And the Lord took me as I followed the flock and the Lord said unto me, 'Go, prophesy unto my people Israel.'" Jeremiah 1:5 adds to this truth when God says, "Before I formed thee in the belly I knew thee; and before you came forth out of the womb I sanctified you and ordained you a prophet unto the nations."

Alexander McLaren, a British theologian and bible expositor, in speaking of the pastor, said," If the pastor is to be worthy of his name, he must be called twice by the Spirit of God. Once to personal faith and once to public service, and without both calls he ought not to enter on this high duty."

Through the years, most believers have followed this biblical truth by viewing their pastor as a man with a divine calling from God. Because of this call, when the pastor speaks the Word of God, the authority actually comes from God. Thus the pastor has authority to fulfill the expectations and duties of his office. Jesus's statement in John 12:48-49 offers further clarification: "He that rejecteth me, and receiveth not my words, has one that judgeth him; the word that I have spoken, the same will judge him in the last day for I have not spoken of myself; but the father which sent me, he gave me a commandment, what I should say; and what I should speak." John Newton, author of the hymn "Amazing Grace" echoed this conviction when he said, "None but He who made the world can make a minister of the Gospel."

Other examples of men called by God were Abraham (Genesis 12), Moses (Genesis 3:1-22 and 4:1-7), Isaiah (Isaiah 6), Jonah (Jonah 1:1-3), and John the Baptist (John 1:6).

Authority conferred by the Bible as the Word of God

Since the Bible is the defining authority of doctrine in faith and practice, all that we do must be true to the Scriptures. We believe the Bible is God's voice from above, far greater than anything men can say. They agree with Augustine, a pastor and bishop in North Africa during the third century, who said, "The preacher explains the text; if he says what is true, it is Christ speaking."

Numerous times in the Old Testament, different prophets wrote, "The Word of the Lord came unto me," such as in Jeremiah 1:4 and Ezekiel 3:16. God has been faithful to give us His written word through scores of prophets and apostles. Therefore when one stands on God's Word, he stands with all the authority of God himself. For this reason people come to church to hear what God is saying to them though the Scriptures.

The Word is very powerful. Paul reminds us in 2 Timothy 3:16, "All scripture is given by inspiration of God, and is profitable for doctrine, for reproof for correction, for instruction in righteousness." Also, "For the Word of God is quick and powerful, sharper than any two-edged sword piercing even to the dividing of soul and spirit, and of the joints and marrow and is a discerner of the thoughts and intents of the heart" (Hebrews 4:12). Therefore when a pastor faithfully preaches the Word of God, it is not his authority – but God's – that should be respected and accepted. "For without me ye can do nothing" (John 15:5).

Authority conferred by the church
as an institution

There is a rich legacy of men who spoke for God. The New Testament writers appealed to and quoted from former prophets for what they were teaching the church. In fact, even Jesus quoted from the Old Testament as a basis for his authority. To stand in that same line of faithful preachers with the prophets and Jesus Christ Himself lends much authority to the credibility of modern-day pastors.

The pastor represents the church, which as an institution that dates back to the time when Christ said, "Upon this rock, I will build my church" (Matthew 16:18). Since Jesus established the church, it is His. Before Jesus ascended to heaven he charged the church with the responsibility to carry out His ministry. All pastors stand upon the foundation laid by apostles like Paul, Peter, John, James, as well as other men of God, like Augustine, Charles Spurgeon, Billy Graham, and tens of thousands of missionaries and ministers of the gospel when they preach. Predecessors have passed on to pastors today a rich heritage of authority.

Authority conferred by the church as an institution is revealed in the ordination of deacons and pastors. In Acts 6, men were chosen to oversee the daily ministry of caring for the practical needs of the church people, "whom they set before the apostles; and when they had prayed, they laid hands on them." The ordination of deacons with the laying on of hands by the church symbolized the transference of authority from the church upon those ordained. For this reason, the Bible gives requirements of specific character traits before men are set aside for the office. Paul further instructed, "Lay hands suddenly on no man" (1 Timothy 5:22) because a man must first prove that he lives up to those requirements. Character requirements are given in 1 Timothy 3 for the ordination of pastors. The authority aspect is seen in Paul's statement concerning ordination of the pastor, "One that ruleth well his own house, having his children in subjection with all gravity; for if a man know not how to rule his own house, how shall he take care of the church of God?" (1 Timothy 3:4-5). Acts 13 records the church choosing Barnabas and Saul for mission work. "Then, having fasted and prayed and laid hands on them, they sent them away" (Acts 13:3). They undertook that mission under the authority of the church.

Authority conferred by the role of the minister

The importance of the role of the pastor is aptly stated in Romans 15:15-16: "Nevertheless, brethren, I have written the more boldly unto you in some sort, as putting you in mind, because of the grace that is given to me of God, that I should be the minister of Jesus Christ to the Gentiles, ministering the gospel of God, that the offering up of the Gentiles might be acceptable, being sanctified by the Holy Ghost."

Martin Luther, in his commentary on Romans, says on the phrase "to the Gentiles" that Paul begins to praise his role, which he had received for the benefit of the Gentiles.

Paul placed high value on the ministry role of the pastor when he wrote to the church in 1 Thessalonians 5:12, "And we beseech you, brethren, to know them which labor among you and are over you in the Lord, and admonish you; and to esteem them very highly in love for their work's sake. Be at peace among yourselves."

The role of the pastor shepherd was important to the writer of Hebrews. He wrote, "Remember them which have the rule over you, who have spoken unto you the word of God: whose faith follow, considering the end of their conversation" (Hebrews 13:7). Both pastor and congregation would do well to recall that Christ is the chief shepherd and, by His supreme authority, has appointed under-shepherds to represent Him. Because of this biblical truth presented in both the Old and the New Testaments, we should seek always to respect and value the role of the under-shepherd.

Therefore, when the church extends a call to a pastor, the church makes the decision for that person to shepherd their church. The person would never be in the place of shepherd leadership in that church apart from the church calling him to be the pastor. With this call, the congregation provides the pastor with authority to carry out the expectations and duties related to the office.

The lack of understanding and adherence to God's role for the pastor as leader has often precipitated staff and other problems. And these problems often have resulted in terminations of staff members and division within the church. It is for these reasons the authors implore the community of faith to be sensitive to the role of the pastor and appropriately protect it.

The following illustration should speak to the need for God's authority structures to be understood and adhered to by the faith community. Many years ago one of the authors visited with a pastor search committee. The previous pastor had left because of a conflict with the minister of music. The committee shared with him that the minister of music had already been informed that if there was conflict with the next pastor, he would be the one terminated.

The setting of this story is most important. The church had built a beautiful thousand-seat sanctuary in colonial-style structure. In the new building, the minister of music had an upscale office suite and an adjacent choir room second to none for rehearsals. The choir room was tiered with individual seats. Nothing was left undone to make the choir suite plush. The parking lot was on the south side of the church. To get to the pastor's office one had to walk from the parking lot across the front of the new sanctuary and across the front of the educational building, to get to the old sanctuary. As one entered the building, there were steps that led down into the basement area to a room that at one time was used as a large assembly room. The assembly room was then being used as a storage room for whatever, and, needless to say, was very junky. On the left side of the hallway leading to that assembly area was the pastor's office. Keep in mind this was in the basement. There was about a foot of window in the pastor's office, but one had to stand up to look out the window, and his view was at the ground level.

He knew where much of the conflict with the pastor and the minister of music lay. He framed a scenario for the committee. A manufacturing company has a plant with a plush office up front in the building and an office in the back of the warehouse. Which one belongs to the president of the company? Their answer was immediate. They replied, "We know we have a problem with the current arrangement." He shared with them that the church was responsible for much of the conflict between the pastor and the minister of music. Furthermore, whomever they called as pastor, there would be further conflict. You cannot give a staff person the sense that he is as important in leadership as the pastor, or, in this instance, practically speaking, more important in leadership than the pastor. As gently as possible, he told them the conflict would continue until the church rectified the office situation.

One is reminded of Aaron and Miriam, who thought they should equally share in the leadership of the nation. Numbers 12 records a sad episode:

> And they said, Hath the Lord indeed spoken only by Moses? Hath he not spoken also by us? And the Lord heard it. (12:2)

> And the Lord spake suddenly unto Moses and unto Aaron and unto Miriam, Come out ye three unto the tabernacle of the congregation. And they three came out. And the Lord came down in a pillar of the cloud and stood in the door of the tabernacle and called Aaron and Miriam: and they both came forth. And he said, Hear now my words: if there be a prophet among

you, I the Lord will make myself known unto him in a vision, and will speak unto him in a dream. (12:4-6)

Not so with My servant Moses; he is faithful in all My house. I speak with him face to face, Even plainly and not in dark sayings; And he sees the form of the Lord. Why then were you not afraid to speak against my servant Moses? (12:7-8, NKJV)

And the anger of the Lord was kindled against them; and he departed. And the cloud departed from off the tabernacle; and behold, Miriam became leprous white as snow, and Aaron looked upon Miriam and behold she was leprous. And Aaron said unto Moses, alas my lord, I beseech thee, lay not the sin upon us wherein we have done foolishly and wherein we have sinned. (12:9-11)

One should be very cautious when being critical of God's servants.

A single voice is God's way of establishing leadership, and hence, authority within any group. God knew Israel did not need divided leadership and established this principle. To ignore or reject this principle results in the diminishing of the effectiveness of the pastor and brings pain to all involved.

As is widely known, there are several ways in which the pastor's role may be adversely affected. Each one should be voided by the family of God in that they are an affront to God and results in varying degrees of pain to His body.

Authority conferred by formal and informal training

Authority is conferred by an educational institution on the basis of training. All vocations expect, and some demand, earned degrees prior to even hiring an individual. The reason is that the training itself gives a person much greater expertise in his field, and with that expertise goes a certain amount of authority. Some vocations require a certain level of formal training. A pastor is in a much better position to receive hearing from the community when he has an earned degree from an accredited university.

However, training can be gained in the school of experience. For proof of this, take a look at the life and ministry of Jesus our Lord. He did not receive formal training in a rabbinical school. A human institution did not give him a degree thus qualifying Him as a teacher. Because Jesus lacked authority given by an institution He ran into opposition. The only time the leading parties of the Pharisees, Scribes, and Sadducees would listen to what Jesus preached was when they were looking for ways to trap Him. Questions were designed to trick Him; they were not designed for learning.

Because of the hardness of their hearts, the religious leaders of that day did not recognize, or accept the presence of God in the person of Christ. Their taking offense at His teachings was so severe that even in the presence of miracles they sought to kill Him, considering Him to be dangerous to the people. This was their plan after the raising of Lazarus from the dead. Their criticism of Jesus carried them to the point of making blasphemous statements because the miracles Jesus performed were obviously the work of God, but they called those miracles the work of the devil. One should ever be extremely cautious, when seeing the work of God in performing miracles and then say that the devil did it. To them, Jesus was nothing more than a carpenter from Nazareth untrained in theology. What authority did He have to do and say the things He did? Jesus was questioned about His authority when He cleansed the temple. Much of the rejection He received was on the basis of His not having conferred authority from the rabbinical institution of His day.

As was true of Jesus, there are many ministers today with little or no formal education. Hence, they are without the benefit of authority conferred by way of formal raining. There is, however, a level of conferred authority by informal training. Though Jesus did not have formal training, He received His authority from God the Father. God had Jesus to be born of a virgin and to be ordained as Messiah. As Messiah, Jesus came into the world to bring salvation to sinful men. It follows then that informal training gained by experience gives the pastor a level of authority that should be recognized and respected.

Most within the faith community recognize that what was true of Christ and His authority is also true of His under-shepherds. However, there are a few in some congregations who are either unwilling to accept this truth or are ignorant of it. This was the case of the disgruntled member who was criticizing the preaching of his pastor. The pastor listened patiently and, at the appropriate time, asked the member if he may ask him some questions, to which the member replied in the affirmative.

"Have you ever preached a sermon?"

"No," replied the member.

"Perhaps you have conducted a funeral?"

"No," replied the member.

"Have you ever counseled a person with a serious problem?"

"No," replied the member.

"Surely you have performed a wedding ceremony?"

"No," replied the member.

"You have no doubt been to a conference or seminar for training as a pastor?"

"No," replied the member.

"Have you ever surrendered your life to the Gospel ministry?"

"No," replied the member.

"Have you ever met and talked to a pastor search committee?"

"No," replied the member.

At this point in the conversation, the pastor said to the disgruntled member, "I have done all of these and much more over the years and you are trying to tell me what and how to do it? Surely, you jest!"

Formal training in an institution or informal training by experience gives persons in all vocations a level of authority that is recognized and respected. The same recognition and respect should apply to the pastor.

Authority conferred as a servant

A minister is to be a servant to the congregation. The more he serves his congregation, the more authority he is granted by the people he serves. On the contrary, the less he exhibits servanthood, the less authority they will in turn give him. Paul and James identified themselves as servants of Christ. "Paul, a servant of Jesus Christ" (Romans 1:1). "James, a servant of God and of the Lord Jesus Christ" (James 1:1). By identifying themselves as servants, Paul and James confirmed they were carrying out the wishes of their master. In the same way, if the pastor is serving Christ as master, the church will more easily recognize his authority.

Allow us to illustrate the value of serving in the context of a husband-and-wife relationship. In Ephesians 5:23, the Bible declares that "the husband is the head of the wife even as Christ is the head of the church; and He is the savior of the body." How was Jesus the savior of the body? He died for the body. The Scripture goes on to say, "Husbands love your wives just as Christ also loved the church and gave Himself for it" (Ephesians 5:25). Jesus saved the church by sacrificing Himself for it and pastors should serve the church in like manner. The husband demonstrates servant leadership to his wife by sacrificing himself for her, and thereby he is the savior of his family. What woman will not accept the leadership of her husband over the home when he sacrifices himself for the family? If anyone is to sacrifice or be sacrificed, it is the husband. Therefore, greater authority is granted to the husband by the wife because of his willing sacrifice for her. His leadership is not only accepted but elevated, because she knows that he will strive to place her and her interest above his own.

Jesus defined leadership in the attitude and role of a servant. Though Jesus was head of the church, He demonstrated His leadership by serving the church. In Philippians 2:6-7 the Bible states in referring to Jesus, "who, being in the form of God thought it not robbery to be equal with God: but made himself of no reputation and took upon him the form of a servant." In Mark 10:45, the Bible says, "For even the Son of man came not to be ministered unto, but to minister, and to give his life a ransom for many."

In the same way, the pastor is to be the leader of the church. He is called by a number of names, such as overseer and shepherd, but he is to fulfill his leadership role as a servant.

Authority conferred monetarily

Paul spoke of giving double honor to the man who labors in the Word. "Let the elders that rule well be counted worthy of double honour especially they who labour in the word and doctrine" (1 Timothy 5:17). Some interpret this as a man who is diligent in his work should be adequately paid. But another interpretation comes from the language Paul used.

The idea of a double portion goes back to the Old Testament laws of inheritance. Those laws dictated that upon the death of the father, the oldest son in the family would receive twice as much inheritance as any other member of the family. This "double portion" conferred on him the authority to lead the family. This was a major way of conferring leadership to the oldest son.

Nelson's Bible Dictionary identifies the birthright as "a right, privilege or possession to which a person, especially the firstborn son, was entitled by birth in Bible times." Part of the firstborn's benefits also was a special blessing from the father and the privilege of leadership of the family. The Bible affirms this was the followed practice among God's people. "But he shall acknowledge the son of the unloved wife as the firstborn by giving him a double portion of all that he has, for he is the beginning of his strength; the right of the firstborn is his" (Deuteronomy 21:17).

The heart of the problem between Esau and Jacob was that the double portion was the right of the firstborn. "But Jacob said, 'Sell me your birthright as of this day.' And Esau said 'Look, I am about to die; so what profit shall this birthright be to me?' Then Jacob said, 'Swear to me as of this day.' So he swore to him, and sold his birthright to Jacob" (Genesis 25:31-33).

A double portion also denoted leadership as in the case of Elisha and Elijah. "And so it was when they had crossed over, that Elijah said to Elisha, 'Ask! What may I do for you, before I am taken away from you?' And Elisha said, 'Please let a double portion of your spirit be upon me'" (2 Kings 2:9). Elijah had established a school of the prophets, and Elisha was to assume the responsibility for leadership in that school after Elijah was gone. This responsibility led Elisha to request a double portion of Elijah's spirit to fall upon him. After Elijah had granted Elisha's request it was clear to the sons of the prophets that the spirit of Elijah did rest upon Elisha because of the way they greeted him by bowing to the ground. "Now when the sons of the prophets who were from Jericho saw him, they said, 'The spirit of Elijah rests on Elisha.' And they came to meet him, bowed to the ground before him" (2 Kings 2:15). The mantle of Elijah fell on Elisha when Elijah was taken up to heaven, and the double portion of his spirit established the authority of Elisha as the successor of Elijah's ministry.

Just as double portions were used to confer authority in Old Testament times, Paul used this same concept to describe pastoral authority in the church. First Timothy 5:17 speaks of the one who labors in the Word is to be counted worthy of double honor. The one who labors in the Word is the pastor, and the church should not doubt his authority to lead the congregation. How is that leadership role conferred? Paul used the same Old Testament concept when he said "double honor." Double portion and double honor have to do with leadership in a specific group. While the Old Testament law has to do with leadership in the family, Paul's "double portion" has to do with leadership in the church. Since not every pastor deserves double honor, Paul qualifies that the benefit be given only to the elders who rule well. Not every pastor will rule well, and need not be counted worthy of double honor.

In order to fully understand the meaning of the word *honor*, a word study of its usage is helpful. The Greek word for honor is *timas*. Several references show that *timas* is to be understood as "monetary compensation." An earlier context of 1 Timothy used the word (*timas*) *honor* in relation to the church's taking care of widows who were not financially able to care for themselves. "Honor [*timas*] those who are widows indeed" (1 Timothy 5:3). In that section, *timas* clearly refers to monetary help. If a widow had family, they were to assume the first responsibility in her care "and let not the church be charged" (1 Timothy 5:16).

Matthew 27:6 records that – Jesus having been sold for thirty pieces of silver – the money was not to be put into the treasury because it was "the price [*timas*] of blood." Acts 4:34 refers to those "who were possessors of lands or houses sold them, and brought the prices [*timas*] of the things that were sold" to the apostles. Ananias and his wife kept back part of the price (*timas*) when they laid the money at the apostles' feet Furthermore Stephen, in his defense recorded in Acts 7:16, references the bones of Jacob being buried in the sepulcher that Abraham had bought for a sum of money (*timas*).

Words have uses as well as meanings. Often one takes a word and uses it freely to express ideas similar to its original meaning. Such is the case for the word *timas*. However, rather than dismissing other connotations from the root, the original meaning can be traced through those usages. The original meaning always lies behind another usage. For instance, the term *timas* can be used in a general sense of the price of a thing, as in 1 Corinthians 6:20: "For ye are bought with a price [*timas*]: therefore glorify God in your body, and in your spirit, which are God's." The price Jesus paid for the sin of the world was His life. We use the term *honor* with the same connotation as *money* in a colloquial expression. A speaker is given an *honorarium* as payment for services rendered. The word *honorarium* comes from the root of *honor*.

Now we come back to Paul's instructions in 1 Timothy 5:17. Paul, the brilliant first-century theologian, was no casual writer. He would not be speaking in one area and then illustrate his point with something entirely different. "Let the elders that rule well be counted worthy of double honor. Thou shalt not muzzle the ox that treadeth out the corn. And the labourer is worthy of his reward" (1 Timothy 5:17-18). The second statement about the worker deserving his wages proves that Paul was talking about money. Otherwise, his illustration and the Old Testament quote are contradictory. What is the meaning of the muzzling of the ox as it treads out the corn? The ox has a right to eat of that which it helps to produce. The worker deserves his wages is clear enough.

Clearly, Paul was addressing financial compensation for the pastor. As believers, we are a people of the book. Since we are not afraid of the Bible, we should let the Bible speak. It is not for us to seek to explain away the clear statements of Scriptures, or to spiritualize them so as to make them lose their meaning. A man who is charged with the responsibility of the spiritual life and development of the congregation also should be seen in light of what Paul says in 1 Corinthians 9:11: "If we have sown spiritual things for you, is it a great thing if we reap your material things?" The comparison is that material things are of far less importance than spiritual things. Said another way, the spiritual things far outweigh financial compensation the church could provide for the pastor. Paul's instruction to give double honor to the pastor is consistent with the authority of the oldest son in the family being given twice the inheritance of any other sibling. The principle of leadership and authority is established in both of them.

The application of this principle will probably create a great deal of discussion because it will be a new idea to many readers. Also, keep in mind that this book is written to address the problem of churches firing their pastor. Although many reasons exist for firing a pastor, the lack of understanding of authority structures on he part of both the congregation and many staff people is one that appears often.

The authors encourage the personnel, budget and finance committees, and other leaders within the family of faith to consider Paul's admonition of "double honor" when considering their pastor's annual remuneration.

In addition, an appeal is made to the state conventions and similar entities to be sensitive to the teaching of Paul in 1 Timothy 1:17-18 when conducting their annual pastor and staff surveys. There is always the danger of the personnel, budget and finance committees, and other leaders averaging together the highest salaries across the state and allowing the average to determine the salary for their pastor. We encourage those persons in charge of these studies at the state level to consider this biblical mandate as they continue to assist the churches in this vital area.

<insert image 255.jpg>

Authority that is earned

The second source of authority is earned. The Bible says, "And it came to pass, when Jesus had ended these sayings, the people were astonished at his doctrine: For he taught them as one having authority, and not as the scribes" (Matthew 7:29). As discussed previously, Jesus did not have conferred authority from a rabbinical school. But this certainly did not leave Jesus without authority. He possessed authority by earning it.

Authority earned by character

Volumes could be written about the character of Jesus Christ. He was the express image of the Father. "He that hath seen me hath seen the Father" (John 14:9). Jesus said also, "Believe me that I am in the Father and the Father in me" (John 14:11). No greater moral authority exists than God the Father. Whom would you trust, the man of truth or a man who is a known liar? Would you want to be under the authority of the man who is totally selfish, seeking his own interests, or the man who has your interest at heart?

Character matters! "When the righteous are in authority, the people rejoice: but when the wicked beareth rule, the people nourn" (Proverbs 29:2). High moral character is a must for a leader. Jesus had authority by virtue of His character. The same must be true of the pastor.

Authority earned by spiritual power and influence

The power of spiritual influence is a further dimension of the authority of Jesus. Coming down from the Mount of Transfiguration, Jesus was met by a man possessed with a demon. The disciples could not cast out the demon, but Jesus did. When the disciples asked why they were unable to cast out the demon, Jesus answered, "Howbeit, this kind goeth not out but by prayer and fasting" (Matthew 17:17-21).

The spiritual impact of a man's life is what gives him personal authority in the minds of people. In keeping with his Christ like character, the pastor's authority grows out of his personal walk with the Lord. Paul's theology of "Christ in you" (Colossians 1:27) is the secret of personal power. The authority of spiritual influence is further reflected in Paul's statement: "Whom we preach, warning every man, and teaching every man in all wisdom; that we may present every man perfect in Christ Jesus. Whereunto I also labour, striving according to his working, which worketh in me mightily" (Colossians 1:28-29). Paul spoke in a number of instances of the power of God working mightily in him.

What a powerful summary Paul gives of the Lord Jesus manifesting himself through his followers. Neither a minister, nor anyone else, can bless anyone. Christ is the one who blesses people through his followers. Listen to Paul's summary:

Always bearing about in the body the dying of the Lord Jesus that the life also of Jesus might be made manifest in our body. For we which live are always delivered unto death for Jesus sake, that the life also of Jesus might be made manifest in our mortal flesh. So then death worketh in us, but life in you.

Jesus blesses others through his servants who are willing to die to self in order that Christ may manifest himself to others through him.

Hence, the authority of spiritual influence is due to the power of God working in the minister's heart and life. Listen to Paul once again: "I am crucified with Christ: nevertheless I live; yet not I, but Christ liveth in me: and the life which I now live in the flesh I live by faith in the Son of God, who loved me, and gave himself for me" (Galatians 2:20). In the minister's life, self is crucified, Christ lives in him, and the power of God working mightily through him results in great spiritual influence. Hence, spiritual influence is the ultimate reality of the lordship of Christ, the completeness of servanthood, the essence of death to self, and the utter obedience to the Holy Spirit by the pastor.

Authority earned by being a servant

We have dealt with this concept of servanthood in the topic about "conferred authority" but it is earned authority as well. The Bible testifies of our Lord that "even as the Son of man came not to be ministered unto, but to minister, and to give his life a ransom for many" (Matthew 20:28). Paul admonished the church at Philippi to "look not every man on his own things, but every man also on the things of others" (Philippians 2:4). That is, each person should do what is for the good of others. Would people on the receiving end of this kind of behavior not grant authority to the man who acts in this way?

Jesus had a discussion with his disciples about authority.

You know that the rulers of the Gentiles lord it over them and those who are great exercise authority over them. Yet it shall not be so among you; but whoever desires to become great among you, let him be your servant. And whoever desires to be first among you, let him be your slave, just as the Son of Man did not come to be served, but to serve, and to give His life a ransom for many. (Matthew 20:25-28)

The way to lead with authority is by way of being a servant. There is a definite correlation between the higher place of authority and the level of serving. Jesus told the disciples; if you want to be greatest of all, that is, you want to be highest in authority, then you be the slave of all.

The story has been around for a long time about George Washington, the father of our country.   He came upon a man whose wagon was stuck in muddy water. Dismounting his horse George Washington walked right into the muddy water and helped the man get his wagon out of the mud. Upon remounting his horse a fellow officer said, "I would never have done that." Washington replied, "I know that," and rode away. That may be one of the reasons Washington was the general.

In a small county seat town church, a young man surrendered his life to preach the gospel. Sometime later, the pastor invited the young man to preach his first sermon. The Sunday came, and the young man marched proudly into the pulpit, read his text, started to speak, and then his mind went blank.   Dejected and embarrassed he walked slowly off the platform. The pastor got up went to the pulpit, and said to the young man, "Son, if you had walked onto the platform in the same manner you walked off of it, you would have no doubt preached a fine sermon."

Once again, alluding to the stories of Esau, Jacob and Joseph is a great illustration of this truth. Jacob and his mother, Rebekah sought to thwart the plans of God. Esau, the firstborn, had the birthright which conveyed the authority for leadership in the family upon the death of Isaac. God had told Isaac and Rebekah when the twins were born that the "elder shall serve the younger" (Genesis 25:23).   Rebekah could not see how that would be possible. However it seems that God wanted to show the world through Jacob that the way of leadership and authority was by way of serving. Though Jacob failed in that servant role, God taught that truth to the world through his son Joseph. In every way and in every relationship, Joseph showed himself to be a servant – whether to the butler, the baker, Potiphar, Pharaoh, or ultimately to the people. Joseph, though a slave, was made manager over Potiphar's business affairs because of his great servant spirit. He eventually became prime minister of Egypt with full authority over Egypt's affairs.

The more a pastor demonstrates the spirit, attitude, and action of a servant the more authority he earns from the people. He needs all the authority he can secure, and an important means of securing that authority is ultimately to assume the role of a servant. Thus, this becomes an authority that is earned.

Because authority and servanthood are interconnected and indispensable to the success of the pastor, utmost caution must be given to protecting it. The Old and New Testament both often used the word *deceive,* which means to mislead, to beguile, to divert attention, to impose upon, or to delude. John reminds us of Satan as a deceiver (Revelation 12:9), and Jeremiah warns, "The pride of thy heart has deceived thee" (Jeremiah 49:6). As is well-known, in recent years the use of *executive* before the word *pastor* has become popular. The authors feel compelled to sound a note of concern with the use of this adjective in association with the word *pastor.* The scripture uses the term *chief shepherd* in reference to Christ. However this term is used to set Christ apart from all others which may not always be the case with today's use of *executive.* Concern with the use of this word and similar ones is expressed because *executive* does not easily attach itself to *servant,* that is, "executive servant." The same may be said of the modern-day use of the word *specialist* to designate a denominational servant. Please note that this is in reference to pastors, not to denominational administrative leadership levels.

Part 2

THE CHURCH'S BIBLICAL RESPONSIBILITIES TO ITS PASTOR

To accept its pastor as a man with a call from God

Paul tells his readers in Romans 16:3-4 about two people who helped him in his ministry. "Greet Priscilla and Aquila my helpers in Christ Jesus: who have for my life laid down their own necks; unto whom not only I give thanks, but also all the churches of the Gentiles." Paul does not go into specifics but points out that these two members of the faith community were helpers, not distracters to his ministry for Christ and the Kingdom. But the most important question is not what Priscilla and Aquila did to help Paul. The question that needs to be asked now is, what is the church doing to help its pastor? Exodus 17:8-12 tells about the children of Israel beginning their journey into the wilderness where they wandered for forty years. As they began their journey, the Amalekites a wicked nation, attacked them. The Lord commanded Moses to carry the Rod of God and for Joshua to lead the battle against the Amalekites. Moses was o lift the Rod toward heaven, giving attention and credit to God or the victory over the enemy.

After a time, Moses's arms grew tired. He began to struggle to keep his arms raised. As long as he was able to lift his arms Israel was winning the battle, but as his arms fell to his side, the Amalekites began to prevail. When Moses's arms dropped, two men of God – Aaron, Moses's brother, and Hur, the son of Caleb – moved alongside and held up Moses' arms for him. Their strength and energy became his. With those two helpers the Rod of God was held high, and Israel won the victory over Satan, or, in this instance, over the Amalekites. Most of us cannot be on the front lines for God like Moses. But we can be like an Aaron and Hur. Some might think what these two did was not all that important. However the role they played in God's plans was the difference between victory and defeat for the nation of Israel. It was William Carey, a great missionary, who said, "I will go into the well if you will hold the rope."

There are myriads of ways people can be an Aaron or a Hur to the pastor as he is lifting high the banner of Jesus Christ. As a community of faith, what members choose to do may be the difference between a church going forward or backward. Standing beside the pastor as Aaron and Hur did with Moses, is much more than a privilege. As Christians, we are commanded by God to recognize and respect the pastor's God-given authority.

Paul asked in Romans 10:14-15, "And how shall they hear without a preacher? And how shall they preach except they be sent?" Paul is underscoring at least two important facts here. One, it is impossible for one to be able to preach unless he be sent; and two it is impossible for one to hear without a preacher.

God spoke to Jeremiah in 1:5, "Before I formed thee in the belly I knew thee; and before thou camest forth out of the womb, I sanctified thee and I ordained thee a prophet unto the nations." Who can doubt that Jeremiah received a specific call from God to perform a specific task?

God called Isaiah: "Also, I heard the voice of the Lord saying, Whom shall I send and who will go for us? Then said I, Here am I, send me. And He said, go and tell this people, Hear ye indeed but understand not; and see ye indeed but perceive not" (Isaiah 6:8-9).

God called Amos: "And the Lord took me as I followed the flock, and the Lord said unto me, go, prophesy unto my people Israel" (Amos 7:15).

God called Paul: "Paul, an apostle of Jesus Christ by the will of God (Not of men, neither by man but by Jesus Christ and God the Father)" (Galatians 1:1).

God called John: "There was a man sent from God whose name was John" (John 1:6).

Failure to see the pastor as a man with a divine call, and to respond accordingly, takes the edge off his spiritual authority and may result in serious consequences – some of which may be eternal. For example, 2 Chronicles 36:15-16 reveals, "And the Lord God of their fathers sent them by his messengers, rising up betimes, and sending; because he had compassion on his people, and on his dwelling place: but they mocked the messengers of

God and despised his words and misused his prophets, until the wrath of the Lord arose against his people, till there was no remedy."

As a faith community, let us obediently accept the biblical responsibility to receive our pastor as a man with a divine calling from God.

To receive its pastor's spiritual teachings

The pastor is obligated by God to provide spiritual teaching. This is explicitly stated in Acts 20:28, "Take heed, therefore unto yourselves, and to all the flock, over which the Holy Spirit has made you overseers, to feed the church of God." God promised Israel that He would give them pastors who would feed them when He said, "And I will give you pastors according to my heart, who shall feed you with knowledge and understanding" (Jeremiah 3:15).

There are other examples of God's command to His pastors to feed His people.

> He saith to him the second time, Simon son of Jonas, loveth thou me? He said unto him, Yea, Lord; thou knoweth that I love thee. He saith unto him, feed my sheep. (John 21:16)

> The pastors which are among you I exhort ... feed the flock of God which is among you, taking the

oversight thereof, not by constraint, but willingly; not for filthy lucre but of a ready mind. (I Peter 5:1-2)

Son of man, prophesy against the shepherds of Israel, prophesy, and say unto them, Thus saith the Lord God unto the shepherds: Woe be to the shepherds of Israel that do feed themselves! Should not the shepherd feed the flocks? Ye eat the fat and ye clothe you with the wool, ye kill them that are fed: but ye feed not the flock. The diseased have ye not strengthened, neither have ye healed that which was sick, neither have ye bound up that which was broken, neither have ye brought again that which was driven away, neither have ye sought that which was lost; but with force and with cruelty have ruled them. (Ezekiel 34:1-4)

God intended His divine call to empower the pastor to put food on the table for the flock. The pastor, in this sense is viewed as a chef; and as a chef it is his God-given duty to serve those who come to dine. As members of the community of faith, let us eagerly partake of the food placed on the table, as we hear and do what the pastor teaches.

To follow its pastor's spiritual leadership

The pastor also is under obligation to God to provide leadership to the church. "One that ruleth well his own house, having his children in subjection with all gravity; for if a man know not how to rule his own house how shall he take care of the church?" (1 Timothy 3:4-5). Paul here contrasts the pastor's ability to preside over his family with his ability to preside over the house of God. If he cannot perform the lesser by ruling his own household, how shall he be expected to perform the greater, by ruling the house of God?

There are many examples of God's commands that indicate the pastor ought to provide leadership. "Take heed, therefore, unto yourselves, and to all the flock, over which the Holy Ghost has made you overseers?" (Acts 20:28). Some translations read "rulers." "Feed the flock of God which is among you, taking the oversight therefore, not by constraint, but willingly" (1 Peter 5:2). "Remember them which have the rule over you, who have spoken unto you the word of God: whose faith follow considering the end of their conversation" (Hebrews 13:7). "Obey them that have the rule over you and submit yourselves; for they watch for your souls as they that must give account that they may do it with joy, and not with grief: for that is unprofitable for you" (Hebrews 13:17).

The apostle Paul expressed concern that the family of faith be faithful and consistent in their lifestyle when he wrote, "And we beseech you, brethren, to know them that labour among you, and are over you in the Lord, and admonish you; and to esteem them very highly in love for their works' sake. And be at peace among yourselves" (1 Thessalonians 5:12). "Let the elders that rule well be counted worthy of double honor, especially they who labour in the word and doctrine" (1 Timothy 5:17).

As a faithful member of the community of believers, we must lovingly accept the biblical responsibility to submit ourselves to the spiritual leadership of the pastor.

To provide adequate financial support

This subject has been adequately treated in a previous chapter.

To safeguard its pastor's reputation

Paul states in 1 Timothy 5:19, "Against an elder receive not an accusation, but before two or three witnesses." We are forbidden by the Holy Scriptures to listen to another person make derogatory or negative remarks about the pastor. Satan often tries to bring the church to a screeching halt by getting church members to say, "Our pastor is a good man, but ..." Instead of listening to someone criticize the pastor, we should pray for him and lead others to do the same. Inasmuch as your pastor has been given the responsibility to proclaim the gospel of Christ, we owe him our prayer support.

God desires the pastor's reputation be protected, but God is just as protective of all his children.

Touch not mine anointed, and do my prophets no harm. (Psalm 105:15)

But let your communication be, "Yea, yea; Nay, nay; for whatsoever is more than these cometh of evil." (Matthew 5:37)

Keep your tongue from evil and thy lips from speaking guile. (Psalm 34:14)

The hypocrite with his mouth destroys his neighbor. (Proverbs 11:9)

He that keepeth his mouth keepeth his life: but he that openeth wide his lips shall have destruction. (Proverbs 13:3)

If any man among you seem to be religious, and bridleth not his tongue, but deceiveth his own heart, that man's religion is empty. (James 1:26)

For he that will love life, and see good days, let him refrain his tongue from evil and his lips that they speak no guile. (1 Peter 3:10).

As part of the faith community, let us conscientiously accept the biblical responsibility to safeguard the reputation of our pastor.

To accept its pastor as a human being

While the pastor has a divine message and a divine mission, he himself is still a human being. The temptation is to view the pastor too highly or to view him too lowly. For example, the Bible introduces Christ's forerunner, John the Baptist, as "a man sent from God" (John 1:6). Paul had this fact in mind when he wrote, "But we have this treasure in earthen vessels" (2 Corinthians 4:7). The treasure of the gospel is perfect, but the earthen vessels of men have multitudes of limitations. Another biblical example of this truth is seen in Peter's response to Cornelius, who "fell down at his feet, and worshipped him." Peter said to Cornelius, "Stand up, I myself also am a man" (Acts 10:25-26).

Let us gladly accept the responsibility to see our pastor as a human being who has a divine message and a divine mission, but one who has definite limitations. Moreover, the pastor must accept himself as a human being and therefore be willing to receive correction.

The pastor has imperfections

Though the pastor should be respected and honored as God's spokesman, he is not God. Paul's instruction is appropriate. "And we beseech you, brethren, to know them which labor among you, and are over you in the Lord, and admonish you, and to esteem them very highly in love for their work's sake" (1 Thessalonians 5:12-13). Ministers are often referred to as reverend, but truthfully, the only one to be revered is Jesus Christ. The pastor is a man just as other men. In accepting the pastor as a human being, people understand he has the same emotional, physical, and mental needs as other men. He is not perfect, but he does represent God to people in a special way.

The pastor is capable of mistakes

Some place the pastor on a pedestal as if to say he is above other men. He is a special representative of God for the special calling to bring God to people. He provides leadership for the people as he faithfully carries out his ministry. There is no leadership without people following. Spiritual leadership has to do with being and doing what is right. Then the people will trust him; and in trusting, they will follow. This is why the Bible gives us qualifications for a person serving as a pastor. His character must be above reproach if his work is to be right. The congregation should not follow him simply because he is the pastor. He must be consistent with Scripture as well so the people will have no problem in following. Everything he does must be based in Scripture. That way, when he is wrong theologically, the church should not follow, but actually make corrections. There are ministers, unfortunately, who have approved of sins that are quite obvious. For the people to follow in such cases would be total disregard for the Word of God. Therefore, in following the leadership of the pastor, the church must demand that he be scripturally sound. The congregational leaders must be serious Bible students themselves.

The same can be said if the pastor leads with selfish motivations and interests. To follow under those circumstances is blind obedience. The pastor is capable of making mistakes, and the responsibility of the church is not to perpetuate those mistakes by following blindly.

The pastor should be corrected when wrong

When the pastor is wrong, Paul gave an admonition: "Rebuke not an elder, but entreat him as a father" (1 Timothy 5:1). That means appeals are to be made to the pastor for corrections. This entreaty implies two levels.

The first level is that of confrontation. *Confrontation* is not a bad word. It brings mistakes to the pastor's attention and allows him to make the necessary correction. People show true friendship when this is done. As it says in Proverbs, "Iron sharpeneth iron, so a man sharpeneth the countenance of his friend" (Proverbs 27:17). When Peter was accepting Gentiles for worship only when the Judaizers were not present, but withdrew fellowship from them when they were present, Paul onfronted him before the church for his wrong. Paul could not et that kind of behavior stand. To allow that wrong to stand vould have been to jeopardize not only the fellowship within he church, but also the ministry of that church in the ommunity.

The second level of entreaty is criticism. Since constructive criticism can be helpful, correcting the pastor when ne is wrong should be done because it is for his benefit. The Lord gives us an example through His own way of reproving and or disciplining a believer. "For whom the Lord loveth he chasteneth" (Hebrews 12:6). When the criticism is justified, bring correction by way of entreaty. The Bible says, "Rebuke not an elder, but entreat him as a father" (1 Timothy 5:1). Destructive criticism does just that; it destroys rather than builds a person up. Church people must be careful how they criticize. The pastor who is strong in his own personhood and accepts the fact that he is human will receive criticism that is just.

To love its pastor

Paul tells us, "And we beseech you, brethren, to know them which labour among you, and are over you in the Lord and admonish you; and to esteem them very highly in love for their work's sake. And be at peace among yourselves" (1 Thessalonians 5:12-13). "To know" means much more than respect. It means feeling what he feels, to know his heartbeat, his vision, to experience what he experiences as the pastor. "For

54

the work's sake" means that the high and noble nature of his work alone, the furtherance of God's kingdom, is reason enough for the church to show its pastor love and respect.

Sometimes the pastor is viewed apart from the church family. Though he is the pastor, he is also a member of the body of Christ, and it would be healthy to view him, not just as a pastor, but as a brother in Christ. Maybe it should be said that the pastor must see himself as one of them in the body of Christ.

There are other biblical teachings commanding Christians to love. "For this is the message ye have heard from the beginning, that we should love one another" (1 John 3:11). John informs his readers that before they heard about the Second Coming, heaven or hell, or even the divinity of Christ, they heard first about love.

We know we have passed from death unto life, because we love the brothers. He that loves not his brother abides in death. (1 John 3:14).

And this is his commandment, that we should believe on the name of his Son Jesus Christ and love one another, as he gave us commandment. (1 John 3:23)

This is my commandment, that you love one another, as I have loved you. (John 15:12)

And this commandment have we from him, that he who loves God loves his brother also. (1 John 4:21)

As a child of God and a member of the Christian community, the pastor also is to be the object of our love and acceptance. Therefore, as part of the Body of Christ, may the church people obediently and demonstratively accept the biblical command to love their pastor. As the congregation accepts this responsibility to love its pastor then other biblical responsibilities to the pastor become less difficult to fulfill.

Because of these biblical injunctions, the congregation and pastor should search for ways to solve conflicts. Honest and open communication ought to be pursued and maintained from the very beginning of a pastor-and-church relationship. Church conflicts sap the energy out of both the pastor and the congregation and deflect the church's ministry from the main thing. As someone has aptly said, "Make the main thing the main thing." Although legitimate reasons exist for terminating a pastor there are fewer than many faith communities are generally willing to accept. The pastor must safeguard and maintain the unity of the flock at all cost, remembering that this unity is second only to doctrinal purity. Both parties should remember that it might take generations for a congregation to get over such an ordeal. In the meantime, souls are dying without Christ and going to hell, families are broken and neglected, and ministry in the community and to the nations often comes to a standstill.

Every church should remember God's warning to Israel after they had mistreated His messengers. "But they mocked the messengers of God and despised His words and misused His prophets, until the wrath of God arose against His people till there was no remedy" (2 Chronicles 36:16). In the same way, pastors should remember God's warnings to them as well:

> Son of man, prophesy against the shepherds of Israel, prophesy, and say unto them, Thus saith the Lord God unto the shepherds, Woe be to the shepherds of Israel that do feed themselves! Should not the shepherds feed the flocks? Ye eat the fat, and ye clothe you with the wool, ye kill them that are fed: but ye feed not the flock. The diseased have ye not strengthened, neither have ye healed that which was sick, neither have ye bound up that which was broken, neither have ye brought them that were driven away, neither have ye sought that which was lost; but with force and with cruelty ye have ruled them. (Ezekiel 34:2-4)

The churches that are growing spiritually, reaching people with the gospel of Jesus Christ, expanding the Kingdom of God, and experiencing harmony take seriously their biblical responsibilities to their pastors. It has been consistently proven that churches and pastors who work at building long relationships grow and are more stable than those who do not. Churches that work at sustaining long and strong relationships with their pastor by fulfilling their responsibility to love him bring glory to God and good to mankind. The same can said of the pastors who take seriously their responsibilities to God, to themselves, and to their congregation.

Part 3

<insert image227.jpg>

THE PASTOR'S BIBLICAL RESPONSIBILITIES TO THE CHURCH

The pastor earns authority by fulfilling his responsibilities to the church. Those responsibilities extend beyond what he does, into something he is as a person. What a man does flows out of his inner self. Character determines behavior. Hence, he will fulfill his God-given responsibilities because they are an essential part of his nature.

To be the man of God for the church

The pastor's first responsibility is to himself, that is, to be what he ought to be as a man of God. The man of God is in ministry because of a call from God: "Paul, an apostle of Jesus Christ by the will of God" (Ephesians 1:1). He was called into the ministry because of his faithfulness. "And I thank Christ Jesus our Lord, who hath enabled me, for that he counted me faithful, putting me into the ministry" (1 Timothy 1:12). Therefore, the pastor must live his life pleasing to the Lord: "That ye might walk worthy of the Lord unto all pleasing, being fruitful in every good work, and increasing in the knowledge of God" (Colossians 1:10). Paul spoke about how the love of money leads to all sorts of evil and then said, "But thou, O man of God, flee these things; and follow after righteousness, godliness, faith, love, patience, meekness" (1 Timothy 6:11).

The pastor cannot lead people any closer to the Lord than he is himself. First and foremost, he must be a man after God's own heart. A successful businessman said, "I spend as much time on improving myself as I do on my job." The idea is that if he focuses on improving himself the job will take care of itself. The pastor must meet the qualifications Paul gives in 1 Timothy 3:2-7 to be "blameless, the husband of one wife, vigilant, sober, of good behavior, given to hospitality, apt to teach; Not given to wine, no striker, not greedy of filthy lucre; but patient, not a brawler, not covetous; one that ruleth well his own house having his children in subjection with all gravity … Not a novice … Moreover he must have a good report of them which are without." These qualifications certainly identify pitfalls the pastor should avoid. At the same time the pastor should do as Paul admonished, "But watch thou in all things, endure afflictions, do the work of an evangelist, make full proof of thy ministry" (2 Timothy 4:5).

To pray and minister the word

Giving himself to prayer is the pastor's first act of ministry to the church and community. "But we will give ourselves continually to prayer and to the ministry of the word" (Acts 6:4). "Take heed therefore unto yourselves, and to all the flock over which the Holy Ghost hath made you overseers, to feed the church of God, which he hath purchased with his own blood" (Acts 20:28). The pastor's first responsibility is to himself for spiritual nourishment and only then can he feed the church. A pure heart and life gives much more validity to the gospel he preaches than empty words. Then he is to make preaching the Word a priority in his ministry to "preach the word, to be instant in season and out of season" (2 Timothy 4:2). There are at least four reasons the pastor must preach the Word.

First, he must preach the Word because God assigned that responsibility to him. Secondly, he must preach the Word because it is by the Word that the lost are saved. "Faith comes by hearing and hearing by the Word of God" (Romans 10:17). Thirdly, he must preach the Word because it is by the Word that Christians grow into spiritual maturity. Fourthly, he must preach the Word because the devil fears nothing more than the truth. The temptation experiences of our Lord recorded in Matthew 4:1-11 reveal a great insight. Each time Satan tempted Jesus in the wilderness, Jesus responded by quoting Scripture. After the final temptation, Jesus commanded Satan to leave, and again, He quoted Scripture to him. Satan then left the presence of

Christ and went away. What a powerful lesson for every pastor to follow!

The pastor must always be on the offense in sharing the Word, regardless of roadblocks Satan puts in his way. The Word of God is a major tool in destroying the kingdom of Satan. Sadly, we live in a day when distractions often crowd out time for prayer and Bible study. But there is no greater calling than to be a pastor of a church and no greater responsibility than to preach the Word. Whatever else the pastor does, he must give himself to the ministry of the Word. Nothing else should take precedence over this responsibility. The importance of this is reflected in what one of our seminary professors taught that for every minute in the pulpit, the minister should spend one hour in study.

A word to the man in the pulpit about the sermon! Of all the surveys performed to determine the cause of termination of pastors, not one survey revealed that the preaching of short sermons caused the termination. One of the authors was responsible for chapel programming at the university where he served. He invited a well-known pastor with the gift of memorization to speak. His subject was "The Greatest Sermon Ever Preached." He quoted Christ's Sermon on the Mount. It took him eighteen minutes! Get up, speak up, shut up, and sit down! In doing so, don't shortchange the work of the Holy Spirit.

As a wise pastor said, "If you want a fifteen-minute sermon, I need two weeks to prepare it. If you want a thirty-minute sermon, I need a week to prepare it. If you want an hour sermon, I am ready to start now!" Inspiration and perspiration usually go together! Prepare both the sermon and the heart! Give equal time in preparing the introduction and the closing!

A word to the people in the pew about the sermon: do not allow the music and the sermon, as important as both are, to determine the depth of your worship experience. The sermon and the music are to be aids to worship, not determining factors. Someone might say, "I received nothing from the sermon this morning!" But worship is in the heart! Is it possible that you could be blessed by knowing that the person next to you did?

But should you insist on criticizing the sermon, at least know what it is that you are criticizing. In an unscientific survey performed by the authors, the vast majority of those responding to the survey were unable to give a simple definition of the term *sermon*. The following is a working definition of the term. "A sermon is the exposing of the mind of God through human personality with a view of stirring the emotions, stimulating the intellect, and affecting the will." The emotions may be stirred, the intellect may be stimulated, but unless the will is changed to conform to the will of God, the failure of the sermon may rest with those in the pew, as well as with the one in the pulpit.

To maintain a strong work ethic

The pastor's work ethic should include at least three things: to always do what is right, always do his best, and always do everything in the right spirit.

The pastor is responsible to do what is right. The Bible records many commands to do what is right and just.

To do justice and judgment is more acceptable to the Lord than sacrifice. (Proverbs 21:3)

He hath shown thee, O man, what is good; and what doth the Lord require of thee, but to do justly, and to love mercy, and to walk humbly with thy God? (Micah 6:8)

Flee also youthful lusts: but follow righteousness, faith, charity, peace, with them that call on the Lord out of a pure heart. (2 Timothy 2:22).

He must be a "lover of hospitality, a lover of good men, sober, just, holy, temperate; Holding fast the faithful words he hath been taught" (Titus 1:8). The pastor's code of ethics must be above reproach. The Bible is filled with admonitions, commands, and instructions for the man of God to do what is right in the sight of the Lord. A high standard of morality and ethics, along with diligence in ministry, is a must.

Moreover, the pastor honors the Lord and the church when he does his best in his work.

Be thou diligent to know the state of thy flocks, and look well to thy herds. (Proverbs 27:23)

Whatsoever thy hand findeth to do, do it with thy might. (Ecclesiastes 9:10)

And whatsoever ye do, do it heartily, as to the Lord, and not unto men. (Colossians 3:23)

The hand of the diligent shall bear rule: but the slothful shall be under tribute. (Proverbs 12:24)

Woe to the idol shepherd that leaveth the flock! The sword shall be upon his arm, and upon his right eye: his arm shall be clean dried up, and his right eye shall be utterly darkened. (Zechariah 11:17)

What a masterful stroke of irony in calling the shepherds after an idol. The idol shepherd who, like an actual idol, has eyes but does not see, has ears but does not hear, has hands but does nothing. He offers the people no help or kindness but leaves them destitute. An idol is worthless. The idol shepherd is not only worthless to the flock but to himself as well. Take note of the sword of God's judgment upon his right eye and upon his arm; that causes him to lose the use of both. His arm withers and dries up, so he is powerless to help anyone, and his right eye becomes utterly darkened so that he cannot discern danger to his flock, nor sees where to find relief, nor where to ead them. A blind leader with no power to do anything for the people is the sum and substance of an idol shepherd. The business of the pastor is to take care of the people. He ought to always be doing what the Lord called him to do. Furthermore, doing everything in the right spirit will help the pastor avoid divisive situations. A right spirit is characterized by humility, compassion, and gentleness: "And the servant of the Lord must not strive; but be gentle unto all men, apt to teach, patient" (2 Timothy 2:24-25). "To speak evil of no man, to be not brawlers, but gentle, shewing all meekness unto all men" (Titus 3:2). Having the right kind of spirit in leading the church moves the pastor far away from being a dictator. The congregation will be far more motivated to follow the pastor when he displays such a spirit, as defined by these verses of Scripture.

The authors are aware that denominations have their own form of church governance. It is hoped, however, that much, if not all, within this presentation will be helpful to the reader.

Some denominations have a congregational form of church government, which means that the church is ultimately responsible for decision making. Most churches conduct their business through committees, but major decisions ought to be brought before the church for final approval. A wise pastor should use foresight to know when a decision may present a problem to the church, and adequately prepare the church for making that decision. This will avoid problems before they arise.

The authors are convinced that most churches will make good decisions when they are given adequate information and time to process that information. The pastor certainly should not make major decisions on his own that might cause problems. One of the authors asked his church to raise money for a building project rather than borrow the funds, which meant engaging an outside firm to help for that purpose. He gave the church eight months to make the final decision. The effort was tremendously effective, and the church not only raised the money for the project but increased general budget offerings and mission offerings as well. The church people, having made the decision, became excited about the project and made it happen.

In treating the people with respect in a spirit of cooperation where the pastor and the congregation mutually share in the conduct of ministry, the pastor will be most effective and will be most appreciated by the people.

To do everything with the right motive

Motives matter! One can do the right thing but with the wrong motive and discredit the value of the ministry. The ultimate motive in all Christian ministries is to bring glory to God. "And whatsoever ye do in word or deed, do all in the name of the Lord Jesus, giving thanks to God and the Father by him" (Colossians 3:17). When one does something as unto the Lord, it determines the attitude, spirit, and motive in which it is done. "Whether therefore ye eat, or drink, or whatsoever ye do, do all to the glory of God" (1 Corinthians 10:31). A second major motive is to do ministry for the good of the people. "Again, think ye that we excuse ourselves unto you? We speak before God in Christ: but we do all things, dearly beloved, for your edifying" (2 Corinthians 12:19). A right motive can never be self-serving but to build up the flock. Paul counsels us to "do all things without murmurings and disputing" (Philippians 2:14).

To be truthful

The pastor is responsible to be truthful. The pastor is the person most responsible for unity in the church. God makes this clear in Jeremiah 23:1-2.

> Woe be unto the pastors that destroy and scatter the sheep of my pasture! saith the Lord. Therefore thus saith the Lord God of Israel against the pastors that feed my people: ye have scattered my flock, and driven them away, and have not visited them: behold, I will visit upon you the evil of your doings, saith the Lord.

Other passages teaching this truth include Jeremiah 2:8, 10:21, 12:10, 22:22, 23:2, 50:6; Zechariah 11:17; Ezekiel 34:2-10; Matthew 15:14; Micah 3:11; Ezekiel 22:25-28; and John 10:12. All together, there are twenty-five passages warning spiritual leaders of the danger of not caring for the flock and its unity.

The pastor must be open with no hidden motives or agendas. Otherwise, he is a wolf in sheep's clothing. Paul, writing to the church in Corinth, states, "but [we] have renounced the hidden things of dishonesty, not walking in craftiness, nor handling the Word of God deceitfully; by manifestation of the truth commending ourselves to every man's conscience in the sight of God" (2 Corinthians 4:2). Paul spoke against the dishonest, crafty, and deceitful minister who, by his works, cannot commend himself to the conscience of others.

A minister who goes to a church and hides his agenda until after he becomes pastor, and then seeks to lead the church in a direction he knew beforehand they did not want to go, is deceitful. Often, this deceitfulness divides a church. God will certainly hold a man responsible who brings contention and discord into the church. "These six things doth the Lord hate: yea, seven are an abomination unto him … he that soweth discord among brethren" (Proverbs 6:16,19). The man who operates on deceitfulness and hidden agendas is not worthy to serve as pastor of a church. How can ministry be done with untruthfulness and deceit from the outset?

Paul spoke further of "giving no offense in anything, that the ministry be not blamed, but in all things approving ourselves as the ministers of God" (2 Corinthians 6:3). Likewise, "rejoice not in iniquity, but rejoiceth in the truth" (1 Corinthians 13:6). "Wherefore putting away lying, speak every man truth with his neighbor: for we are members one of another" (Ephesians 4:25). The pastor who is not truthful forfeits ministry to the people and, therefore, the right to be their pastor.

To shepherd the people

The congregation is called of God to be the church, and meeting their needs is of profound importance. The pastor is called of God to be an under-shepherd to the people. Shepherd and sheep are apt analogies for describing the relationship of the pastor to his people. Jesus gave a command to Peter, "Feed my sheep" (John 21:16). In so doing, He has given ministers of every age the same command. One notices that Jesus said, "My sheep." The minister must see that the flock is not his but the Lord's. The people are not objects to be used to obtain a goal. The pastor is responsible to shepherd the church of God. He does not function as a CEO but as a servant to the people. Therefore, he is to lead the sheep, not drive them, as the Bible says, "He goeth before them, and the sheep follow him: for they know his voice" (John 10:4). "The hireling fleeth, because he is an hireling, and careth not for the sheep" (John 10:13). Notice the contrast between the hireling and the good shepherd. "I am the good shepherd: the good shepherd gives his life for the sheep" (John 10:11).

The essence of ministry is service. Paul uses the term "bond slave" to show how a true servant ought to lay aside his own ambitions in order to minister to the flock. He should follow Jesus's example, as recorded in Philippians 2:7: "But made himself of no reputation, and took upon him the form of a servant." A pastor who views himself as a bond slave to the people will not intentionally abuse his authority.

The attitude of a genuine servant is one who seeks to make others successful; hence, the servant pastor focuses on ministering to rather than being ministered unto. A servant is open and responsible to people – to the point of being flexible in order to have an authentic ministry. We can learn from Paul once again when he wrote, "For though I be set free from all men, yet have I made myself servant unto all, that I might gain the more" (1 Corinthians 9:19). Paul was determined not to plunge ahead to have his own way. He made himself a slave in order to reach people and minister to them. God gave a dire warning to pastors who fail in this responsibility:

> Son of man, prophesy against the shepherds of Israel, prophesy, and say unto them, "Thus saith the Lord God unto the shepherds; woe be to the shepherds of Israel that do feed themselves! Should not the shepherds feed the flocks? (Ezekiel 34:2-4)

Paul instructed Timothy in a positive way, saying, "That the man of God may be perfect, thoroughly furnished unto all good works" (2 Timothy 4:17).

Servanthood is a prerequisite to spiritual authority. The pastor succeeds in his role as servant before succeeding as a pastor, since the biblical order is always servant first and spiritual authority second.

To love the people

The pastor is responsible to love the people. Love enables a pastor in being an effective minister. "Be kindly affectioned one to another with brotherly love; in honour preferring one another" Romans 12:10). And "Seeing ye have purified your souls in obeying the truth through the Spirit unto unfeigned love of the brethren, see that ye love one another with a pure heart fervently" (1 Peter 1:22).

Since Paul taught with spiritual authority, we can learn from his example. He speaks of himself using analogies of a caring nurse and an affectionate father.

As an affectionate nurse, he says, "But we were gentle among you, even as a nurse cherisheth her children: So, being affectionately desirous of you, we were willing to have imparted unto you, not the gospel of God only, but also our very own souls, because you were dear unto us" (1 Thessalonians 2:7-8).

As a father, Paul said, "As ye know how we exhorted and comforted and charged every one of you, as a father does his children" (1 Thessalonians 2:11). Paul's leadership style came from his heart.

In summary, the seven responsibilities of the pastor are the following: to be a true man of God, to give himself to prayer and the ministry of the Word, to maintain a strong work ethic, to do all things for the right motive, to be truthful, to be an under-shepherd to the people, and to love the people. The pastor needs to learn to deal with helpful criticism by being humble, by a willingness to learn, and by a willingness to listen.

A church will find it extremely difficult to dismiss a pastor who fulfills these responsibilities in the spirit of Christ and for the glory of God.

Part 4

<insert image071.jpg>

THE MOTIVATION NEEDED
TO OBEY GOD'S AUTHORITY

This chapter is about the motivation needed to obey and honor God's authority. Without this motivation, little will be accomplished, but with it, miracles can become a way of life.

For the growing believer, love is not an option. The means by which we can accomplish God's love is by following the example of Christ Himself who laid down His life on the cross. He said, "As I have loved you, that ye also love one another" (John 13:34). But there is more. Paul writes in Romans 5:4, "The love of God is shed abroad in our hearts by the Holy Ghost which has been given to us." God has given the believer the Holy Spirit to enable him to fulfill this command to love. If we have difficulty in loving others, the Holy Spirit is not in control of our lives. As believers, we need to pray for God to fill us with the Holy Spirit so that we will truly be a channel of His love to all around us. We should not ignore the fact that the first sermon ever preached centered on love. "For this is the message

74

you have heard from the beginning that we should love one another" (1 John 3:11).

Love may not make the world go round, but it does make the trip much more enjoyable. The place and need for love cannot be overstated. The Bible asserts, "God is love" (1 John 4:16). Jesus spoke often about the need for love in the life of every believer.

Life is a series of choices, including the decision to love. The decision is ours, and the Bible is filled with examples of those who chose to love and those who chose not to love at all. Love changes people. Unfortunately, too many of us are like two young brothers who were fighting each other when Mom walked into the room, pulled them apart, and said to the eldest, "Now you tell your brother you are sorry!" The older brother responded after a moment, "I will in a minute, Mom, but first, can I hit him one more time?" Amazing how that inclination lurks within all of us. Love is a major foundation of the home.

Similarly the church's biblical responsibilities to the pastor and the pastor's biblical responsibilities to the church are the foundation stones of the church family, hence the motivation to obey God's directives are fulfilling those responsibilities in love.

WHO ARE WE TO LOVE

God has commanded us to love individuals and groups. First of all we are to love Jesus. God is most interested in how believers feel toward Him. For example, more than once, Christ asked Peter if he loved Him (John 21:15-17). John gave a valid reason for loving Christ with our all when he wrote in 1 John 4:19, "We love him, because he first loved us." Also, we are told to "love the Lord your God with all your heart, with all your soul, and with all your mind" (Matthew 22:37).

Other Scriptures teaching believers to love Jesus include the following:

And you shall love the Lord your God with all your heart, and with all your soul and with all your might. (Deuteronomy 6:5)

Keep yourselves in the love of God. (Jude 1:21)

I love you O God. (Psalm 18:1)

By this we know that we love the children of God, when we love God, and keep His commandments. (1 John 5:2)

Secondly, we are told to love others. The parable of the Good Samaritan in Luke 10:25-37 teaches that one's neighbor is anyone in need, not just those next door or those within a certain friendship circle. Jesus adds in the Sermon on the Mount, "For if ye love them which love you, what reward have ye? Do not even the publicans the same?" (Matthew 5:46). Christ is calling for a depth, breadth, and height of love that is all-inclusive.

> Seeing you have purified your souls in obeying the truth through the Spirit ... see that ye love one another with a pure heart fervently. (1 Peter 1:22)

> Love the brotherhood. (1 Peter 2:10)

> By this shall all men know that ye are my disciples that ye love one another. (John 13:35)

> Beloved, let us love one another, for love is of God and everyone that loveth is born of God, and knoweth God. (1 John 4:7)

> Beloved, if God so loved us, we ought also to love one another. (1 John 4:11)

Loving others also includes loving one's enemies.

> But I say unto you, Love your enemies, bless them that curse you, do good to them that hate you, and pray for them which despitefully use you, and persecute you. (Matthew 5:44)

But love ye your enemies, and do good, and lend, hoping for nothing again; and your reward shall be great, and ye shall be the children of the Highest: for he is kind unto the unthankful and to the evil. (Luke 6:35)

Other scriptures commanding us to love others include 1 John 4:20-21; Matthew 5:43-46; 1 John 5:2; 1 Peter 4:8; 1 John 2:9-10; and 1 Thessalonians 4:9-10.

Moreover, Jesus commanded us to love the church. It is a biblical fact that the church is the body of Christ. Therefore to love Christ is to love His church. It is incorrect to say, "I love Jesus, but I do not care for the church." Just as Christ showed His love for the church by dying for it, His example should be enough to cause believers to love it too. We are to love the family.

God intended for love to start in the family. The fifth commandment reads, "Honor thy father and thy mother, that thy days may be long upon the land which the Lord thy God giveth thee" (Exodus 20:12). This commandment is pivotal because the last five commandments relate to those outside the family, and if love does not begin in the home, it will not extend to the outside world. Therefore, love in the family is of supreme importance.

Wives, submit yourselves unto your own husbands, as unto the Lord. (Ephesians 5:22)

So ought men to love their wives as their own bodies, he that loveth his wife loveth himself. (Ephesians 5:28)

Children, obey your parents in the Lord: for this is right. Honour thy father and mother; which is the first commandment with promise: That it may be well with thee, and thou mayest live long on the earth. And, ye fathers provoke not your children to wrath: but bring them up in the nurture and admonition of the Lord. (Ephesians 6:1-4)

Other scriptures teaching family members to love each other include Jeremiah 13:20; 1 Peter 3:7; Titus 2:4; Ecclesiastes 9:9; Malachi 4:6; 1 Timothy 5:8; Genesis 1:27-28; Matthew 19:4-5; and Luke 16:18.

Furthermore, we are to love the lost. Christ proclaimed the purpose of His earthly ministry when he quoted, "The Spirit of the Lord is upon me, because he hath anointed me to preach the gospel to the poor; He hath sent me to heal the brokenhearted, to preach deliverance to the captives, and recovering of sight to the blind, to set at liberty them that are bruised, to preach the acceptable year of the Lord" (Luke 4:18-19). Jesus would say later to His disciples, "As my Father has sent me, even so send I you" (John 20:21). Our mission is to continue the ministry of Jesus in loving the lost. Paul said, "My heart's desire and prayer to God is that Israel might be saved" (Romans 10:1). "The fruit of the righteous is a tree of life; and he that winneth souls is vise" (Proverbs 11:30). We should remember well that "God commendeth his love toward us, in that, while we were yet sinners, Christ died for us" (Romans 5:8). Other Scriptures instructing us to love the lost include John 20:21; Matthew 28:18-20; Luke 14:21; Acts 1:8; 2 Corinthians 5:20; and Romans 9:1-3.

Also, we are to love the minister of Christ. Christ is often referred to in Scriptures as the Chief Shepherd. The pastor is referred to as the under-shepherd. The minister is the visible representative of the invisible Christ on earth. "And we beseech you, brethren, to know them which labour among you, and are over you in the Lord and admonish you; and to esteem them very highly in love for their work's sake" (1 Thessalonians 5:12-13). "Obey them that have the rule over you, and submit yourselves: for they watch for your souls, as they that must give an account, that they may do it with joy, and not with grief: for that is unprofitable for you" (Hebrews 13:17). Other Scriptures instructing us to love the minister of God are Mathew 23:37 and 2 Chronicles 36:15-16.

We are to love ourselves. Since we are created in God's image we can have confidence in the person God made us to be. He knows that even though we ought to view ourselves in the light of His grace we often do not. One's love for others is predicated upon his love for self. "Jesus said unto him, Thou shalt love the Lord thy God with all thy heart, and with all thy soul, and with all thy mind. This is the first and great commandment. And the second is like unto it, thou shalt love thy neighbor as thyself. On these two commandments hang all the law and the prophets" (Matthew 22:37-40). Loving oneself does not mean being selfish. It means self-affirmation, a sense of self-worth, which comes from being created in the image of God.

The importance of love of self cannot be exaggerated. Jesus placed it alongside loving God with all one's heart as one of the two commandments upon which all else depends. Through years of counseling and observing people in personal relationships, one comes to understand how vital love of self is in sustaining relationships. It is one of the greatest needs of the human heart. It has to do with self-affirmation. A person with low self-esteem, and hence a very negative self-image, has difficulties in personal relationships. This personality deficiency, more than almost anything else, will make it extremely difficult for a person to sustain strong relationships. If one feels that he himself is not worthy to be loved, then in his mind and spirit, no one else is worthy to be loved. One who has a negative self-image seeks to compensate for it by seeking to make himself look better than others. Personal relationships begin to suffer. This is the kind of person who needs to be the center of attention. He needs to be in control because control gives him a sense of importance. He needs to brag on himself. He needs to put other people down to make himself look bigger. It is all about him. He is the major focus. He is not free! He is insecure in his personhood, and he is bound emotionally to making himself look like somebody. He is not able to tolerate correction or, especially, criticism. All these expressions of a lack of loving self will affect immensely personal relationships.

One sees the power struggle among the twelve apostles as Jesus was moving toward the last days of His life and they were expecting Him to set up His kingdom. They were arguing about who would have the honored positions; there even was a request that two of them sit on the right and on the left of Jesus in His kingdom. They all were seeking importance through having the most honored positions. This kind of power struggle will adversely affect any and all relationships. They were caught up in a power struggle to gain affirmation by a sense of being the most important one.

Rather than getting one's self-concept from other people, that is, what he thinks they think of him, one should get his concept of self from God. God made each person unique, and hence, each is already a person of high value. John 13 records a very interesting episode of Jesus washing the disciples' feet. In their insecurity about themselves, not one of the disciples would stoop to wash the feet of the others. Oh, that would make him look less than the others, and their egos would not tolerate that position. But "Jesus knowing that the Father had given all things into his hands, and that he was come from God and went to God; He riseth from supper, and laid aside his garments; and took a towel, and girded himself … and began to wash the disciples' feet" (John 13:3-5). Knowing that He came from God and was going back to God had everything to do with His sense of security in self-identity. What difference did it make what others thought of Him? Hence, He was free to do the most menial task because He had himself off His hands. He was not caught in a struggle to be somebody or to make himself look important. He was already somebody! Jesus had 100 percent self-affirmation. He was totally secure. He did not have to prove himself to anyone.

This is a plea for all pastors and church people alike to earnestly seek the face of God in accepting themselves as God made them so they will be free to do anything and everything in ministry no matter how menial the task may be. Jesus was free to be a servant! The pastor must be free to be a servant if he is to succeed in ministry. Church people must be free to be a servant to minister effectively. Jesus was absolutely right; all that a minister does hangs on him loving God and loving himself.

Also, we are to love the children and the youth. The need for believers to have a deep, consistent love for children is implied in the example of our Lord. While it is true He loves everyone, in Mark 10:13-15, the Scripture singles out this important age group as having a special place in His love and care. "And they brought young children unto Him, that he should touch them: and his disciples rebuked those that brought them. But when Jesus saw it, he was much displeased, and said unto them, Suffer the little children to come unto me, and forbid them not: for of such is the kingdom of God. Verily I say unto you, Whosoever shall not receive the kingdom of God as a little child, he shall not enter therein."

Other scriptures singling out children as a group whom Christ loves include Luke 13:15-17 and Matthew 19:14.

In Mark 10:17-22, a beautiful story is told of the rich young ruler who approached Christ. He wanted to know what he had to do to have eternal life. When Christ told the young man to give all to the poor and put God first, the young person was not willing to do so. As he turned and walked away, the Bible says, "Then Jesus beholding him loved him" (Mark 1:21).

The congregation and the pastor who passionately love Jesus, love the church, love others, love the family, love the lost, love the under-shepherd, love themselves, love children, and love young people are manifesting to the world they have a respect for and obedience to the authority of God.

BIBLICAL REASONS FOR LOVING

We may not understand fully the Second Coming, predestination, or election, but the Bible's teachings about loving one another are unmistakably clear. God's love in the believer's life makes it possible to have respect and obedience for God's authority. Christians are to love people at all levels of society. For example, 1 John 3:11 says that love was the message heard from the beginning. Peter stated it this way, "And above all things have fervent charity among yourselves" (1 Peter 4:8).

People go to the grocery store for groceries, to the shoe store for shoes, to the gas station for gas, and to the Christian and to the church for love and acceptance. What if there were no groceries at the grocery store, no shoes at the shoe store, and no gas at the gas station? The same disappointment comes when unbelievers find Christians that do not show love. As a community of faith, let us determine we will reflect Christ's love to everyone.

Every person needs to be loved:
A necessary reason for loving

Food, clothing, and shelter! These are the basic physical needs of every human being. In the same way, the need to be loved and accepted is also a need of all ages and races. Christ recognized this need by making every person He met an object of His love. The woman at the well, little children, the thief on the cross, and many others had this need satisfied as He lavished His love on them.

May God give us grace as believers to learn how to get past race, titles, and sin in the lives of others, by showing the love of God! Many in the world are not healthy emotionally, physically, or spiritually, and one reason might be due to a lack of our loving them. Flowers must have water to be healthy. In a similar fashion, human beings who are created in the image of God need love and are incomplete without it. When the lost person and immature believer meet the followers of Christ, they expect to find love. If they do not find love in the lives of church people, where else are they to find it? Let us do our best not to disappoint them in their search.

Christ commanded it:
A demanding reason to love

One of the most difficult tasks Christians have is to love all mankind. Yet the Bible teaches that God commands us to love one another. Over and over Christ urges His followers to do as He did. For example, Christ says, "A new commandment I give to you, that you love one another. As I have loved you, so you are to love one another" (John 13:34). Thus, believers have a commandment to obey: "love one another," and an example to follow: "As I have loved you that you also love one another."

Love for one another is God's will. "And this is his commandment that we should believe on the name of his Son Jesus Christ and love one another, as he gave us commandment" (1 John 3:23). John asserts also, "And this commandment we have from Him that he who loves God loves his brother also" (1 John 4:21). The verb form indicates a continuous attitude. Furthermore, this continuous love may be viewed as a basic test of one's commitment to Christ Himself. Lack of love for one another is proof we lack also authentic love for Christ. Remember also that this commandment to love our brother is from Him, that is, Christ Himself.

"If you love me, keep my commandments" (John 14:15). The depth and sincerity of a Christian's love for Jesus is indicated by his keeping the commandments of Christ. If we love Him, we will keep His commandments. If we do not love Him, we will not keep His commandments. And what does our ord say in John 14:24? "These things I command, that you ove one another."

Much of our worship today can be as false as it was in the days of the prophet Ezekiel. "And they come to you as the people come, and they sit before you as my people, and they hear your words, but they will not do them: for with their mouth they show much love, but their hearts go after their covetousness" (Ezekiel 33:31).

Loving is the means of becoming Christ like: A majestic reason to love

Have you ever prayed or heard someone pray, "O Lord, please make me more like Christ"? What do you suppose would be God's response to that prayer? "Oh, so you want to be more like My Son, do you? If you mean it, you may want to start by loving others."

One of the attributes of God is love, and if we are sincere in our desire to be godly, we must remember we are never more like Him than when we express love.

John writes in 1 John 4:12, "No man has seen God at any time. If we love one another God dwells in us, and his love is made perfect in us." First, John asserts that no one has ever seen God. However, John says it is possible to view God through the love we display to others. When people see our love for each other, John says they are given a picture of the real character of Jesus. The world has no idea what God looks like. But as we look past barriers caused by race, gender, weakness, and past sins, and truly love others as God does, the world will catch a glimpse of God.

Loving is evidence of the New Birth: An indispensable reason to love

Some people doubt their salvation. Without being judgmental, if you could observe the way they fail to demonstrate love, you would doubt their salvation too. Imagine if a woman in a traffic jam was arrested, booked, and jailed. Later, at her trial, the judge set her free and asked the policeman why he arrested her in the first place. The policeman explained, "Your Honor, she was yelling, cursing, and using unfriendly gestures. However, on the car she was driving were stickers that read, 'Honk if you love Jesus!' and 'Turn or burn,' and 'Always follow the Golden Rule.' I arrested her, Your Honor, because I assumed she was driving a stolen car."

John writes in 1 John 2:9, "He that says he is in the light, and hates his brother, is in darkness even now." Disdain for others nullifies any claim to Christian discipleship. John believes that loving others proves one has a walk with Christ. He states this truth in 1John 3:10, "In this the children of God are manifested, and the children of the devil: whosoever does not do righteousness is not of God, neither he that loves not his brother." The distinguishing characteristic of a Christian is not church membership, baptism, tithing, or even witnessing. But

According to Christ, this is the distinguishing mark of a Christian: "By this shall all men know that you are my disciples if you have love one to another" (John 13:35).

Finally, John states that love toward others confirms the believer's relationship to the Lord. "Beloved, let us love one another, for love is of God, and everyone that loves is born of God and knows God" (1 John 4:7). What would you think of a person who claims to be a football player but knows nothing of football? What would you think of someone who claims to be a farmer but has never farmed? Loving as Christ loves gives credence to the believer's claim of a walk with God.

Obligations must be paid:
An essential reason to love

We all appreciate God's love. After all, where would we be without it? But this amazing love must not only be appreciated but imitated as well. John teaches this important truth in 1 John 4:10-11. "Herein is love, not that we loved God but that He loved us, and sent His Son to be the propitiation for our sins. Beloved, if God so loved us, we ought to love one another."

John expounds on this fact in 1 John 3:16. "Hereby perceive we the love of God because He laid down His life for us: and we ought to lay down our lives for the brethren." In this verse, John teaches that the essence of love is self-sacrifice. The phrase, "He laid down His life" means literally to "divest oneself of a thing." A person's life is his most precious possession. Christ dying for our sins shows He divested Himself for us so that we might be saved and go to heaven. The Bible teaches that the followers of Christ should imitate His act of self-sacrifice. In laying down our lives, we prove our love for others. On the other hand, not to lay down our lives is evidence that our love is not real and any confession of love for others is but empty boasting.

Seldom, if ever, are we called to give our lives for another. However, we constantly have opportunities to give lesser gifts, such as forgiveness, prayers, care, and financial aid. Christ's ultimate gift of love for us obligates us to give expressions of love to others.

Love enables us to forgive and move on: A beautiful reason to love

How can we relate properly to a person who has offended us? Repentance and asking for forgiveness by the offender certainly would help. Otherwise, we must depend upon God's love, which alone has the power to enable us to forgive those offenses. Love in our hearts from the Holy Spirit gives us the strength to forgive and move on with our lives.

Peter provides this valuable insight, "And above all things have fervent charity among yourselves: for charity covers the multitude of sins" (1 Peter 4:8). There are two possible interpretations to this passage Peter could be saying that as we love one another, God forgives us of our sins. On the other hand,

e may also mean that love helps us overlook sins in the lives of
ur neighbors. The word *cover* means "to throw a veil over;
understand what we cannot approve; conceal what normally we
would condemn." To accomplish this feat, Peter reminds us we
must be willing to "have fervent charity among ourselves."

Furthermore, God's example motivates us to forgive our
neighbor's offense against us. God, in love and mercy to us,
throws a veil over our sins, understands what He does not
approve, and conceals what normally He would condemn.
Likewise, we must do the same as followers of Christ.

Forgiveness is important for another reason, as Jesus
teaches in Matthew 18:32-35.

> Then his lord, after he had called, said to him, O you
> wicked servant, I forgave you your debts, because
> you desired me to: should not also have you had
> compassion on your fellow servant, even as I had
> pity on you? And his lord was upset, and delivered
> him to the tormentors, till he pay all that as due him.
> So, likewise shall my heavenly Father do also to you,
> if you from your hearts forgive not every one his
> brother their trespasses.

God's forgiveness of our sins is directly related to our
forgiveness of those who have sinned against us.

Such forbearance of another's sins and faults often
promotes harmony, aids the healing process, and fosters spiritual
growth. If we want such an attitude exercised toward us by our

Heavenly Father, we must not refuse it to others. This forbearance of another's wrongs is applicable only when the honor of God and the well-being of the Body of Christ are not at stake, or when love itself would require another course of action. The beauty of love is that it enables us to forgive another's faults, because God has already forgiven us for our own.

All opportunities to love will soon be gone: An urgent reason to love

The time will come quickly when all opportunities to love will forever be gone, lost in the dark ocean of yesterday. If one plans on loving, if one has a notion to love, now, this moment, is the time to begin doing it, because no one knows how much time he will have left.

Sometimes the motivation for sending flowers in memory of a person is to make up for not giving flowers to that person while they were living. The authors want to say something most all of us feel is true in our hearts. It is this: if you want to give anyone flowers, give them while they can enjoy them, because "dead noses smell no roses."

Many people are moved by David's cry for his son, "Oh, Absalom, my son, my son, Absalom. Would to God I had died for thee, oh, Absalom, my son, my son" (2 Samuel 18:33). This stirring expression of love by a father, however, fell upon deaf ears. Absalom was dead. David's cry of love for his son came oo late. David's sobs were useless, because Absalom was out n the countryside, hanging from a tree limb by the hair of his lead, killed by David's commanding general, Joab.

If Absalom could have spoken from the dead, he might have said, "Dad, I don't want you to weep for me, but I'll tell you what I wish you had done. I wish you had taken me fishing. I wish you had found time to play a game or two of ball with me." David's tears of heartfelt love, though real to himself, were of no consequence to Absalom. Earlier, yes. But not anymore. David's opportunities to love his son were forever gone.

Before Absalom's death, David had banished him from Jerusalem. He had killed his half brother Amnon because he had raped Tamar, Absalom's full sister. Absalom fled and was gone for three years. What adds to the heartache of this story is that it did not have to be that way. David had not seen Absalom for those three years. Recall the day David said to Joab, his commanding general, "Go therefore, bring back the young man Absalom" (2 Samuel 14:21). The officer left and found Absalom and brought him to Jerusalem where David lived. Even then, the Bible says, "So Absalom dwelt two full years in Jerusalem and saw not the king's face" (2 Samuel 14:28). The question that begs an answer is why? David may have been too busy to express love to his son. Or it might have been that David was bitter toward Absalom for killing Amnon for the rape of Tamar (2 Samuel 13:28-29). Neither explanation justifies David's failure to love his son.

Has someone been a blessing to you? Tell them. Has someone been a source of strength or a role model to you? Tell them! Don't wait until it is too late. Do it while still you are able. Opportunities to express love will soon be gone. Give God's love to everyone you can while you still have the opportunity.

Oscar Hammerstein II, an American writer and theatrical producer, wrote,

A bell's not a bell till you ring it –
A song's not a song till you sing it –
Love in your heart was not put there to stay –
Love isn't love till you give it away!

Love is not easy because it is often very costly. The more one loves, the more vulnerable he becomes, and the deeper will be his hurts. Love identifies with another in their needs. Consider what it cost God to love a broken and sinful humanity. Love is not simply an emotion; it is a command that is our obligation to accept from the Lord. Hence, it is action! Love is demonstrated by what one does: "For God so loved the world that He gave his only begotten son" (John 3:16), and that Son died for the sins of the world. How do we know that God and Jesus love us: because He was willing to die for us. The command is one that we cannot fulfill on our own, but can fulfill with the help of Christ living within us. "I am the vine, ye are the branches: He that abideth in me, and I in him, the same bringeth forth much fruit: for without me ye can do nothing"

John 15:5). Love is produced in cooperation with the Holy Spirit: "But the fruit of he Spirit is love, joy, peace, longsuffering, gentleness, goodness, faith, meekness, temperance" (Galatians 5:22-23).

The results are the same whether you choose one, two, or more of these reasons to love. Others will be encouraged, invigorated, and you will be blessed here; and hereafter, your example will reflect obedience to Christ's authority, and God will be glorified. Equally important, your obedience and respect for the authority of God will be a shining light for others to follow.

Part 5

A GLIMPSE OF THE BEAUTY OF UNITY AND PEACE

THE CONGREGATION AND MINISTER AT THEIR BEST

When the community of faith and the under-shepherd recognize the value of authority that is conferred and earned, and the congregation honors its biblical responsibilities to the congregation, and both are motivated to love all persons and groups in obedience to His authority, a spectacular and beautiful picture of unity and peace emerges. The purpose of this final chapter is to share with the reader what that picture looks like.

An Old Testament writer provides a glimpse of this picture. Psalm 133:1 says, "Behold, how good and how pleasant it is for the brethren to dwell together in unity." The psalmist exclaimed "Behold" as he viewed this magnificent wonder. He was overwhelmed by what he saw! He may have told his friends later, "This wonder is worthy of your inspection. Come and see it!" What overwhelmed his senses was the unbelievable beauty of the unity and peace existing between brothers and sisters in the faith. The beauty is encompassed in the words *good* and *pleasant*. What he saw – unity and peace – is characteristic of the followers of Christ.

There are valid reasons he called his unity good and pleasant. First, the unity is good and pleasant for all the members. It is neither fair nor right for the vast majority of the membership to suffer because of a small minority. Second, the unity is good and pleasant for the under-shepherd and other leaders in the faith community. It is neither reasonable nor right for the pastor and others to get caught between opposing groups. Third, the unity is good and pleasant because it indicates the overall health of the body of Christ; and with the exception of doctrinal purity, nothing is as important as the unity of the community of faith. Fourth, unity is good and pleasant because it indicates that Jesus is Lord of the church. *Lord* means "master" or, in modern terms, "boss." Being Lord or boss enables Christ to bless the ministry of the church and His presence will beautify its every part! Little wonder the psalmist exclaimed, "Behold"!

The apostle Paul said to the church at Thessalonica, "And ye become followers of us and of the Lord, having received the word in much affliction, with joy of the Holy Ghost: so that ye were examples to all that believe in Macedonia and Achaia" (1 Thessalonians 1:6-7). Paul links the church's exquisite and vivid "example to all believers in Macedonia and Achaia" to their being "followers of us and of the Lord" and thereby revealing their obedience and respect to the authority of God. It was a great compliment to the church for Paul to refer to them as a role model for so many other Christians. The compliment was justified because of the unity and peace that existed within that community of faith. What a legacy for succeeding generations to imitate!

It was for this cause that Paul challenged the church at Ephesus with this statement: "With all lowliness and meekness, with longsuffering, forbearing one another in love; Endeavoring to keep the unity of the Spirit in the bond of peace" (Ephesians 4:2-3). Paul and other biblical writers encouraged and exhorted the church to exhibit unity and peace.

> I appeal to you, brothers and sisters, by the name of our Lord Jesus Christ, that all of you agree, and there be no divisions among you, but that you be united in the same mind and the same judgment. (1 Corinthians 1:10, ESV)

> Do nothing from rivalry or conceit, but in humility count others more significant than yourselves. (Philippians 2:3, ESV)

> [Be] eager to maintain the unity of the Spirit in the bond of peace. (Ephesians 4:3, ESV)

> I entreat Eudora and I entreat Syntche to agree in the Lord. (Philippians 4:2, ESV)

The hand of God was also on Judah to give them one heart to do what the king and princes commanded by the word of he Lord. (2 Chronicles 30:12, ESV)

Finally, be ye all of one mind, having compassion one of another, love as brethren, be pitiful, be courteous: (1 Peter 3:8)

Every faith community must be cognizant of and stirred deeply within their spirits by our Lord praying repeatedly for the unity and peace of His church. Not once, nor twice, but five times in the Lord's Prayer in John 17 Christ prayed for its unity! "… that they may be one, as we are" (v. 11). "That they all may be one;" (v. 21). "… that they all may be one in us" (v. 21). "… that they may be one, even as we are one" (v. 22). "… that they may be made perfect in one …" (v. 23).

The Corinthian church was conflicted with a four-way party division: Paul, Apollos, Cephas (Peter) and Christ parties. Paul addressed the issue with strict, straightforward, bold language. "Now this I say, that every one of you saith, I am of Paul; and I of Apollos; and I of Peter; and I of Christ" (1 Corinthians 1:12). In the Greek language, the person is in the ending of the verb. One does not need any additional word to indicate the person. But in this verse Paul intensified his appeal to the church by adding the personal pronoun "ego" in each of the phrases, plus he added an intensive particle in the first phrase, and then a strong adversative in the last three phrases. If one translated verse 12 as written by Paul, the verse would read as follows: "I, indeed I, I am of Paul: but, I am of Apollos; but I am of Peter; but I am of Christ." One can readily identify the root problem. Paul was saying the heart of the Corinthian havoc was self-elevation, which is the opposite of Christ's qualifications for being one of His disciples. "And he said to them all, if any man would come after me, let him deny himself, and take up his cross daily and follow me" (Luke 9:23). Later, in 1 Corinthians 43:1, Paul would call these believes "babes in Christ." That was not a very pretty picture then, nor is it now!

One can appreciate beauty more when contrasted with what is ugly. Good can be appreciated more when contrasted with bad. Peace can be appreciated more when contrasted with disharmony or war. A picture of unity, harmony, and peace in the church is therefore appreciated far more when contrasted with division. A spirit of self-denial, which promotes unity and peace, can be appreciated more when contrasted with self-elevation, which promotes disunity and broken relationships. "Blessed happy) are the peacemakers: for they shall be called the children of God" (Matthew 5:9).

All believers have the responsibility to make the prayer of our Lord for unity in John 17 a reality. In so doing they give credence to the pastor's conferred and earned authority. They also give evidence of the fulfilling of the church's biblical responsibilities to the pastor as do the pastors their fulfilling of their responsibilities to the church. Of equal importance, they give validity to the importance of being motivated to authentically loving all persons and groups. Thus, they reveal their obedience and respect to God's authority.

A final word to every believer: in your obedience and faithfulness, you help those around you to catch a glimpse of the beauty of unity and peace within the church. One day, the Lord will pronounce an immeasurable blessing upon you for your obedience to His authority in your walk with Him.

CONCLUSION

We have sought to provide some understanding of the nature of the church, especially as it relates to authority. Both conferred authority and earned authority have been explored in depth. The church confers authority on a man called to be pastor essentially because he is called of God and stands as God's representative to the people. But conferred authority must be supported by earned authority. The pastor earns authority by being above reproach and fulfilling major responsibilities. The responsibilities of the church to the pastor and the responsibilities of the pastor to the church have been presented in detail. Furthermore, we have given the motivations needed to obey God's authority and follow pastoral authority. When these responsibilities, both on the part of the pastor and on the part of the church, are fulfilled, the church will experience growth, unity, and peace.

This study gives a framework for understanding church conflicts that often lead to a pastor's termination. This book is not seeking to address the particular approach to resolution of those conflicts except to say that when conflicts arise, they should be dealt with immediately. Leadership in the church must sit down in consultation with a pastor before the problems get out of hand. If this study helps in understanding the place of authority given to the pastor, then wise men of the church will know how and when to address a problem.

The greater the pastor's servant spirit is displayed, the greater acceptance the church will give to his authority, because the church knows he will not abuse it or use it for his own benefit. When the church is thus free in total trust of the under-shepherd to be the pastor leader, his authority will be enhanced.

Jesus Christ is the head of the church (Ephesians 1:22, 4:15, 5:23; Colossians 1:18). He has given major principles to govern the life and work of both pastor and people. The authors have identified those principles. When these are followed the name of our Lord Jesus will be honored because it will be obvious that He is in control of the church.

Dr. Adams served as a pastor over twenty-five years and as interim pastor to thirty congregations. Pastorates include FBC, Springfield, TN and FBC, McKenzie, TN. He holds a BD degree from Union University, and Master of Divinity and Doctor of Ministry degrees from New Orleans Baptist Theological Seminary. He served as Vice-President for Religious Affairs at Union University, from 1982-1999. Adams also taught pastoral ministries, evangelism and homiletics at Union and served as adjunct professor for The Southern Baptist Theological Seminary. He has served as a trustee of institutions convention wide and state wide, including the International Mission Board of the SBC, and Union. Dr. Adams has been married to Robbie for sixty years. They are the parents of two daughters, two grand daughters and four great grand children. They reside in Jackson, Tn.

Dr. Alexander served as a pastor in churches in Tennessee and Mississippi over fifty years. He holds a bachelor's degree from Union University and Master of Divinity and Doctor of Ministry degrees from New Orleans Baptist Theological Seminary. He served as an adjunct professor in Old Testament studies at Union University and Blue Mountain College. He has served as a trustee of various denominational institutions. He retired from the pastorate of First Baptist Church, Tupelo, Mississippi, and still serves churches as an interim pastor. He and his wife, Keliea, have two children and four grandchildren, and still reside in Tupelo.

Made in the USA
San Bernardino, CA
29 July 2018